365

SELF

DISCOVERY

QUESTIONS

MARRIAGE
365

CASEY & MEYGAN CASTON

COFOUNDERS OF MARRIAGE365

Illustration and Design: Sel Thomson
Typesetting: Melanie Etemadi
Back Cover Photography: Haylee Forster

ISBN 978-1-7324358-6-5

Published in 2020 by Marriage365 Media Group

We would like to dedicate this book to our Marriage365 members. You inspire us with your bravery and vulnerability every single day. Each and every one of you is making this world a better place and we're so glad we're on this journey of self-discovery with you all.

CONTENTS

HOW TO USE THIS BOOK

By Date

For each day of the year, there is one question. Turn to the date of the year and begin your self-discovery journey. You don't need to start on January 1st. Any day is great to start. Some people like to commit to one question a day while others prefer to binge several questions in one sitting.

By Topic

If there is a specific area you want to focus on, pick a question by topic using the index (pg. 199) that can be found in the back of the book. If you've had a difficult day, we recommend choosing a question from the JUST FOR FUN category.

As Journal Prompts

We've included several blank pages (pg. 183) at the back of this book for you to write any notes, ah-ha moments, or things that you want to remember for the future. You can also use these pages for journaling or doodling as you move through each question.

WHERE TO USE THIS BOOK

- A book club
- At your workplace
- In therapy sessions
- With a small group of friends
- As a conversation starter with your partner
- For parents - with your teenage or adult children
- As journal prompts (see page 183 for blank pages to journal)
- A daily check-in with yourself

INTRO-
DUCTION

Self-discovery is one of the greatest pathways to building confidence in our lives, but it seems like we are too busy these days to stop and check in with ourselves. We are overwhelmed with demanding work commitments, kids' sport schedules, 24-hour news coverage, the time suck of video games, friends' parties to go to, the latest binge-worthy Netflix show, not to mention the family gatherings and house projects. For most of us, we wake up checking our phone, move through the day, and fall asleep scrolling through social media's endless feeds. These are activities that crowd out our time that allow us to bounce from one distraction to another, and it's killing us. Like a cat with a laser pointer, we chase after the next shiny object that will busy our time. We've lost the art of reflection, gratitude, and awareness.

Let's do a quick exercise to help you reflect, be grateful, and become even more self-aware. First, I want you to take a deep breath and then close your eyes so you can pay attention to what's around you. (Ok, you can peek to read ahead first). Now, bring what you hear to the front of your mind. Is it leaves rustling, music playing, or the not-so-faint noises of children playing in the house? Open your eyes and take a couple of deep breaths. Look around you. What do you see? Is there something that catches your eye that you are grateful for? Now, think about your last interaction with another person. Was it something you are proud of where you both listened and engaged with mutual respect? Or were there hurt feelings and emotional disconnection? There... that was easy. That took maybe a few minutes or less, but you centered yourself, quieted your mind and moved closer to being proactive in your life, rather than reactive.

The journey of becoming self-aware is the process of self-discovery and that starts by asking great questions of yourself.

Self-aware people carry themselves with confidence because they've taken the time to explore who they are and how they want to be known (that is, self-discovery). These people have done the hard work of asking themselves tough questions. They have courageously confronted the lies that they have told themselves like, "I'm not good enough," or "Why try if I'm going to fail?" or "I'm just not smart enough." They've overcome the inevitable childhood baggage and the fears that hold them back. Because of their hard work, these brave souls make a tremendous impact in the lives of those around them.

Insecure and hurting people, on the other hand, often react to life's peaks and valleys as each moment comes, rarely stopping to think about how they show up in life. They run from introspection and avoid dealing with interpersonal conflict for fear that their emotional shallowness could be revealed. Their life is marked by selfishness and emotional laziness because they are too afraid to turn on the lights and expose the fears that have held them back for so long. Sorry (not sorry) if that sounds harsh, but at the core, it's true.

HERE'S HOW SELF-DISCOVERY BEGAN IN OUR LIFE

Early in our marriage, we got into a huge fight about being on time versus being late. We were both angry, hurt, and filled with pride, which meant days of giving each other the silent treatment. Who would break the silence first? Who would apologize first? We finally agreed that we needed to see a counselor since we couldn't even be in the same room without wanting to say hateful and hurtful comments. We sat down on our new counselor's couch feeling nervous and a little excited because both of us were hoping that the neutral party sitting across from us would call the other one out. But what she said rocked our worlds. "So Meygan, can you explain to Casey why being on time is so important to you, where that energy comes from, and how it makes you feel when he's late? And Casey, after Meygan shares, I will be asking you the same question, but I want to know how it makes you feel when she gets upset with you for being late."

Her questions made us both stop and really think about why we cared so much about this fight about being on time versus late. Here were our responses...

Meygan: *Growing up, my parents were always on time, which is a sign of respect when someone is counting on you. Trust is one of my core values and how do I trust someone who I can't rely on?*

Casey: *My home life was chaos. As an only child raised by a working single mom, I was often in day care. There were times I was the last one to be picked up or dropped off late and I had to get over it. Things happen and I think you should make your best effort to try and be on time, but there are bigger problems in the world to worry about.*

As we processed where our value systems came from, we noticed that Meygan's frustration came from one of her core values being challenged. For Meygan, something as simple as Casey being late caused her to feel like he didn't respect her and that she couldn't rely on him, breaking the trust they had built. And for Casey, he felt frustrated because it was unfair that Meygan's negative reaction to a

5-10 minute delay could and often did spoil the time they had together. His value of spending time together and building connection, stemming from abandonment wounds, was more important than promptness. In this one instance, we discovered that rarely is one of us right and the other one wrong, we're just different people with differing views that both stem from our childhood and life experiences.

Our couselor helped us start the journey of self-discovery by asking us great questions: what we felt, why we felt it, where those feelings came from, and how we responded to life when things didn't go our way. It's this journey that we are still on and now invite you into. This book will help move you away from your insecurities into a place of confidence because of your willingness to become self-aware. We want you to dig deep--what you put in is what you get out. We've marked the journey for you with questions, but it's up to you to find time to take the journey.

It's funny because we still occasionally argue about being on time and being late, but at least we know why it's an issue. Our goal is that you would recognize that you have room for improvement because individuals who practice self-discovery are more aware, and self-aware people tend to be healthier friends, co-workers, parents, spouses, and siblings.

WHAT IS SELF-DISCOVERY AND WHY IS IT IMPORTANT?

Personal development has been a growing trend for many years. More and more people are actively looking for ways to improve their lives by having a better understanding of who they are. Many people listen to podcasts, read books, take online personality assessments, attend retreats, or go to therapy so that they can become the best version of themselves.

The self-discovery journey will help you uncover your passions and guide you to identify your motivations and drive. A life void of your passions and strengths is a life without fun, joy, and fulfillment. You will get to dream about what you want your future to be like and turn your desires into real-life stories.

A huge part of personal growth is self-discovery and we believe that it's a lifelong journey of exploring your thoughts, feelings, dreams, concerns, trauma, past experiences, responses, and personality. It's getting you to know yourself better, on a more intimate level. We are always changing and evolving which means that we need to be constant learners of ourselves, requiring us to be more aware.

Becoming more self-aware will also help you discover what you need and desire in relationships with your friends and family. With these questions, you will learn which people bring out the best in you and which bring out the worst. You will begin to recognize which behaviors make you feel insecure and which make you feel empowered. You will discover how to evaluate your expectations of others and what you want your relationships to look like moving forward. Practicing self-discovery will help you feel more confident with and around the people you come across every day.

Self-discovery gives you a chance to heal from past traumas and experiences that you've been holding onto. Life dishes up many hardships like illness, death, abandonment, and heartbreak. Every one of those hurts becomes personal. While shining light on your past can be very emotionally draining, it also starts the process of forgiveness and healing, which you both need and deserve.

WHY DO SO MANY STRUGGLE WITH SELF-DISCOVERY?

The biggeset hurdle is *time.* We move at such a pace where our schedules are filled to the brim, leaving no room for self-care. Many people move through the motions of everyday life without ever stopping to check in with themselves to see what's working or how they're feeling. Another common thing that gets in the way of self-discovery is *fear.* Fear of the unknown and fear of realizing that you're in a toxic relationship. There's fear of having to change unhealthy behaviors and fear of going back to painful memories. There's fear of disappointment and fear of failure. There's fear of exposing your actions and choices from the past and there's fear of shedding light on your thoughts that you feel shame around.

And lastly, oftentimes people have a desire to become more aware but don't have the *tools, resources,* or *support* that they need. This is exactly why we wrote this book and are so glad you picked up a copy. You're putting aside your fears, taking the time, and now have a practical tool to help guide you on this journey of self-discovery.

OUR TOP TIPS FOR MAKING THE MOST OF THIS BOOK

Tip #1

There are no right or wrong answers. With 7 billion people in this world, we're all uniquely made with different upbringings and personalities and there's no shame in that. Your answers reveal how you feel and what you think in a given moment. You may ask yourself the same questions years later and answer differently. Self-discovery isn't effective when you worry about how your response sounds compared to others. We're all on our own journey of trying to learn more about who we are, why we do what we do, and why we think the way we do.

Tip #2

Stay away from minimizing or avoiding pain. A common survival technique is to stuff away any memory that was painful (or shameful) by placing it in a box that we seal up and put away in our attic never to be looked at again. The problem with this is that the feelings attached to that memory will eventually bleed out, usually at an unexpected time and often in an unhealthy way. Stay away from thinking things like, "It wasn't that bad compared to others," or "I don't want to bring it up or I'll open the flood gates." Part of self-discovery is leaning into painful experiences to learn more about how you handled it and how it changed your view of yourself and others.

Tip #3

Get curious. The people who "master" self-discovery are those who aren't afraid to get curious as to why they think, feel, and do what they do. Getting curious shows that you desire to know yourself on a deeper level and that you want to be an emotionally aware and healthy person. Getting out of your comfort zone can be draining and overwhelming at times, but remember to keep making your emotional and mental health a priority.

Tip #4

Don't be your worst critic. It's easy to become the harshest judge of your life choices, taking away from your opportunity to grow emotionally. Have you made mistakes? Of course you have! Because we're all imperfect, messy people who struggle with insecurities, pride, and selfishness. Making yourself feel bad for a choice you've made will only hold you back from moving forward. So, if at any point you notice that you're criticizing yourself and your answers, say any of these statements to yourself:

"Attempting to do this took courage and I'm proud of myself for trying."

"I am capable and strong and I will get through this."

"I can learn from this situation and grow as a person."

"This was an opportunity for me to learn more about myself so I can change my future."

Tip #5

Take your time and put away distractions. Opening this book up minutes before you have a big work meeting or when your kids are tired and hungry is probably not the best idea. This book is not about finishing in record time or rushing through each question as if checking off your weekend to-do list. Self-discovery requires time, patience, and an open mind to really think, process, and meditate on your experiences.

Tip #6

Use the 'Feelings Words List' often. The questions in this book are going to ask about how you feel and we encourage you to expand your emotional vocabulary by using our handy and convenient *Feelings Words List* on page 195. It might be easy at times to answer certain questions without really getting into it. Don't be afraid to dive into the feelings that come up as you share your answers. And if you don't know how you feel about a topic or question, don't be afraid to explore that either (more on this later).

Tip #7

Have fun! Life is hard enough and self-discovery should also be fun and bring joy and laughter to your life. Consider the time you're spending on yourself as a gift. Each time you open up this book and answer a question, smile knowing that you are becoming a smarter, more confident, happier person.

I HAVE NO ANSWER TO THE QUESTION. NOW WHAT?

Here you are, taking time to explore and strengthen your emotional health. You read a question and nothing comes to mind. So you take a deep breath hoping that something will come up, but nothing. It's okay to not recall past memories or specific feelings about a certain topic. Our advice is to skip the question and go to the next one. Mark each question you skip so that you can come back to it on a different day when you have more time, have processed the question on your own, or are in a different headspace.

Be aware that if you have a lot going on personally or professionally, whatever you are going through may be the reason you feel emotionally or mentally stuck. Even the idea of engaging in conversations around self-discovery can be overwhelming and cause stress. If that's what you're feeling, we recommend setting aside time to rest and reset. Designating time for self-care each day will help you make the most of your self-discovery journey. A walk or run, a kid-free cup of coffee, a long shower or a few chapters of that book you picked up months ago-- a little bit can go a long way. Remember, this is a journey, not a race, and we hope you're in it for the long haul.

There are questions that get very specific about sexuality, politics, religion, racism, and other hot topics. If these questions feel big to you or this is the first time you're approaching the subject, that's ok. Start with where you're at, answer as best as you can, and consider circling back when you've had more time to process the question or topic. We encourage this! When done in the spirit of learning and understanding, these potentially sticky conversations can lead to incredible personal growth.

Bonus tip: Not everyone feels inspired by sitting down, reading a question, and then writing down their response. While there are dozens of ways to process and answer these questions, consider thinking and walking. Think of it like active meditation centered around a reflective question. Many people we've worked with have found success taking a walk in nature and repeating the question a few times out loud as they process. You could do this alone or with a friend, family member, confidant, etc.

FEELING TRIGGERED?

A trigger is an emotional wound that reminds you of something you believed to be unfair or unjust in your life. For example, if your parents neglected your emotional needs, this can cause you to feel triggered because you feel that was unfair for them to treat you that way.

Many of the questions you'll find in this book address topics you may have never asked yourself. Going there may bring up new emotions that will make you feel uncomfortable. These emotional triggers are revealing aspects in your life that are unresolved or frustrating to you. Some may be traumatic and even confusing, but the good news is that you're doing the healthy thing by drawing them out so you can start to process and heal.

If you experience a trigger when answering one of the questions, here are some suggestions:

- Take deep breaths. Slow and controlled breathing forces oxygen to the brain and helps calm nerves.
- Get active by taking a walk, going to the gym or for a swim and get your heart pumping. Our bodies produce endorphins when we move, which can elevate your state of being.
- Start journaling. Don't limit yourself to what you should or should not be writing. Journaling is a proactive way to deal with anxiety and triggers and can help you get what you're feeling and thinking out of your mind and onto paper. When you are writing, don't edit or worry about grammar, just be as honest as possible about what you're experiencing.
- Call a safe friend, mentor, pastor, or your counselor. Oftentimes we need to verbally process what we're going through when we feel emotionally triggered. Allowing someone who cares about you into that space

is extremely therapeutic.

- If you feel rushed or are around people, it's ok to give yourself an adult time-out and go back to the triggering question at a later time when you have more space and capacity to dive in.

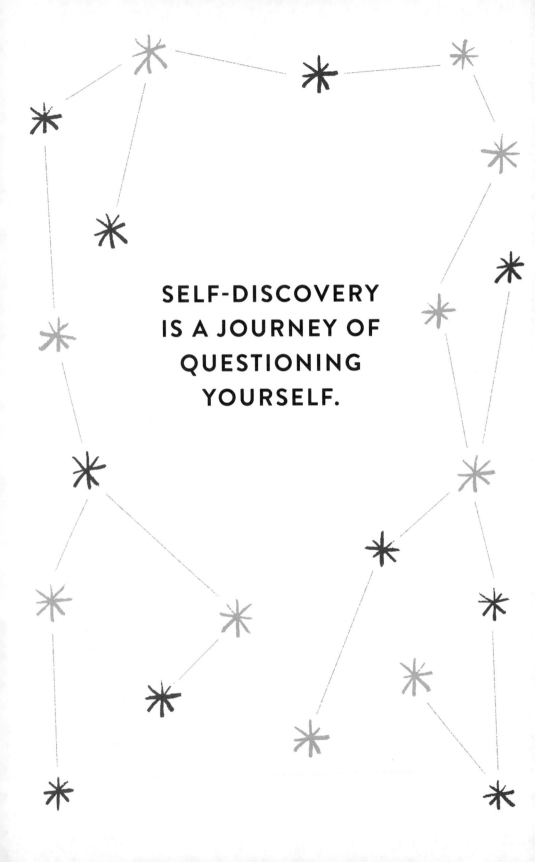

SELF-DISCOVERY
IS A JOURNEY OF
QUESTIONING
YOURSELF.

1

JANUARY

JANUARY 1

Do you think that a sense of humor is essential to a healthy relationship? Why or why not?

JANUARY 2

How can you engage with your local community in a way that you are not currently?

JANUARY 3

If you could write one message on all of the billboards all over the world for one day, what message would you choose?

JANUARY 4

What motivates you when you're feeling
challenged or stuck?

JANUARY 5

Did your family model healthy boundaries
growing up? Why or why not?

JANUARY 6

Is it difficult for you to accept compliments
from other people? Why or why not?

JANUARY 7

Growing up, did you feel safe and secure
most of the time? Why or why not?

JANUARY 8

Do you have a desire to learn more about
yourself? Why or why not? What steps are
you taking to become a better person?

JANUARY 9

What is one thing that people do
not notice about you right away that
you wish they would?

JANUARY 10

What would you change about your
money habits right now and why?

JANUARY 11

What is one behavior that you never
tolerate no matter who it's coming from?

JANUARY 12

When was the last time you felt
vulnerable? Who were you with and how did
you handle the situation?

JANUARY 13

What are two of your favorite memories with your family as a kid? What makes those memories stand out to you?

JANUARY 14

Have you ever felt judged, ignored, or mistreated because of your race? Explain.

JANUARY 15

What is one of the nicest things someone has said to you? How did hearing it make you feel and why?

JANUARY 16

Did you ever have an honest lesson about anatomy, learning about genitalia and its function? If so, who was the person who taught you? Was it accurate? Was it harmful or confusing?

JANUARY 17

Which values do you believe are the most important to keep in mind when it comes to voting?

JANUARY 18

Which quote that you've read inspires you and why?

JANUARY 19

Do you express your gratitude
and if so, how often?

JANUARY 20

Is there anyone in your life you're
holding a grudge against? What do you
hope happens?

JANUARY 21

What was your first job and
what did it teach you about money
and work ethic?

JANUARY 22

What would be your advice to someone
who has lost hope?

JANUARY 23

Do you like surprises or do they
unsettle you and why?

JANUARY 24

How much time do you spend on your phone?
Are you content with the amount of time or
do you need to set healthier boundaries?

JANUARY 25

What emotional baggage do you carry with
you as a result of your childhood?

JANUARY 26

How does stress affect your body?
How can you address this issue?

JANUARY 27

Geographically, where would you like to live
10 years from now and why?

JANUARY 28

How do you handle confrontation with those you care about?

JANUARY 29

What is one area in your life that you are the most proud of and why?

JANUARY 30

If you were to start a nonprofit organization, what need would it solve in your community or in the world?

JANUARY 31

How important is it that you
always look your best and why?

STRIVE FOR
PROGRESS, NOT
PERFECTION.

FEBRUARY 1

Who is the first person that comes to mind if you were asked about the greatest hurt in your life? What thoughts come up when you think about that person?

FEBRUARY 2

Do you think that you are easily influenced by others? Why or why not?

FEBRUARY 3

Have you ever heard stories about anything interesting that happened during or soon after your birth? Explain.

FEBRUARY 4

Do you take the time to reflect on
what is happening in and around you?
Why or why not?

FEBRUARY 5

When it comes to your career, do you
consider yourself someone who is confident?
Why or why not?

FEBRUARY 6

When someone you care about wrongs you,
are you someone who thinks about revenge or
forgiveness or a little of both?

FEBRUARY 7

Who is one famous person, dead or alive,
that you feel like you have the most in
common with and why?

FEBRUARY 8

When was the last time you cried?
What did you cry about?

FEBRUARY 9

Do you consider yourself a sensual person?
Why or why not?

FEBRUARY 10

How many close friends do you want and why?

FEBRUARY 11

What is the value of practicing hobbies?
Do you have a hobby that you love and never want to give
up? Is there a new hobby you'd like to try?

FEBRUARY 12

How do you prefer to celebrate your
birthday and with whom?

FEBRUARY 13

How do you deal with negative people?
Do you think your actions towards them
are helpful or harmful? Think of a specific
example to guide you.

FEBRUARY 14

What is the kindest thing you have
ever done for someone?

FEBRUARY 15

What is your biggest pet peeve?

FEBRUARY 16

Do you enjoy small intimate gatherings with a couple of close friends or do you prefer larger events like parties? Explain.

FEBRUARY 17

Did you find it easy to get along with your peers when you were growing up? Why or why not?

FEBRUARY 18

In your life, what has been the biggest blessing in disguise?

FEBRUARY 19

If you had no deadlines or other
obligations, what project or task would
you focus on right now?

FEBRUARY 20

Who makes you feel anxious? What do they
do that causes you anxiety?

FEBRUARY 21

What are some of the mistakes you made in
past romantic relationships that you regret?

FEBRUARY 22

Do you feel like you live with purpose
and are intentional about the choices
you make? Explain.

FEBRUARY 23

Growing up, did you ever feel let down
by an adult? Explain.

FEBRUARY 24

What comes to your mind when you
think about God?

FEBRUARY 25

Do you have any toxic friends in your life?
How can you deal with this?

FEBRUARY 26

In this last month, did you give yourself the
time and resources needed to accomplish your
goals? Why or why not?

FEBRUARY 27

Do you believe that a certain amount of
money should be set aside for pleasure, even if
you're on a tight budget? Explain.

FEBRUARY 28

What is your favorite Olympic
sport and why?

THERE IS ALWAYS
SOMETHING TO
BE GRATEFUL FOR
WHEN YOU ALLOW
YOURSELF TO BE
FULLY PRESENT IN
THE MOMENT.

MARCH

MARCH 1

Have any past experiences shaped the fears
and anxieties you have today? Explain.

MARCH 2

Do you consider yourself an open-minded or
closed-minded person? Explain.

MARCH 3

Have you ever loved someone who didn't love
you back? How did that make you feel?

MARCH 4

Do you lack energy? If so, what do
you think is the cause?

MARCH 5

Do you know which unhealthy behaviors
trigger you and why? Examples: interrupting,
eye-rolling, closed-mindedness, laziness, etc.

MARCH 6

When was a time when you were generous with
either your money or time? Explain.

MARCH 7

What is something you really did not want to
do that turned out to be a terrific experience?

MARCH 8

What are your thoughts about plastic surgery?
Do you think you will ever make any cosmetic
changes to your body? Why or why not?

MARCH 9

What kind of person do you want to be five
years from now and why?

MARCH 10

Who do you feel safe to be yourself with?
Is there any way you can spend more time
with this person/these people?

MARCH 11

Is there anything in your life that makes you
feel ashamed? Explain.

MARCH 12

At what age do you think it's appropriate to
teach children about sex and their anatomy?
Explain.

MARCH 13

Do you believe what you read and see in the
news, or do you question where information is
coming from and the media's true agenda?

MARCH 14

If you could pick one year of your life to do
over, which would it be and why?

MARCH 15

Have you ever been called a workaholic by
your friends or family members? What are
signs that someone is a workaholic?

MARCH 16

What is your history (past or present) with health issues? Are you concerned about having health issues in your future? Explain.

MARCH 17

What was your favorite holiday as a kid and why?

MARCH 18

Which person in your life is your exact opposite? What makes you so different from one another?

MARCH 19

When was the last time you laughed out loud?
Who were you with and what happened?

MARCH 20

Did your mother, father, or other family
members abuse each other or you in any way?
Examples: sexual, emotional, physical, etc.

MARCH 21

Would you ever be willing to go to counseling
if you or the people in your life felt like you
needed it? Why or why not?

MARCH 22

What is the best financial decision you made
in the past? What made it so great?

MARCH 23

Do people often ask for your help with
something specific? What is that thing and
why do you think they ask you and not
someone else?

MARCH 24

What is the worst piece of advice
anyone has ever given you?

MARCH 25

Have you ever experienced any sexual
trauma in your childhood or adult life? If so,
have you reached out to someone for help?
Why or why not?

MARCH 26

Which political issues do you
care about, if any?

MARCH 27

Have you ever heard the story of how
your parents met? If so, what stands
out to you about it?

MARCH 28

What is your go-to response when someone
you care about hurts your feelings?

MARCH 29

Are you someone who likes to set goals?
Why or why not?

MARCH 30

Have you been emotionally lazy in any of
your relationships? If so, have you apologized?
Why or why not?

MARCH 31

If you could change one thing about the way you looked, what would it be and why?

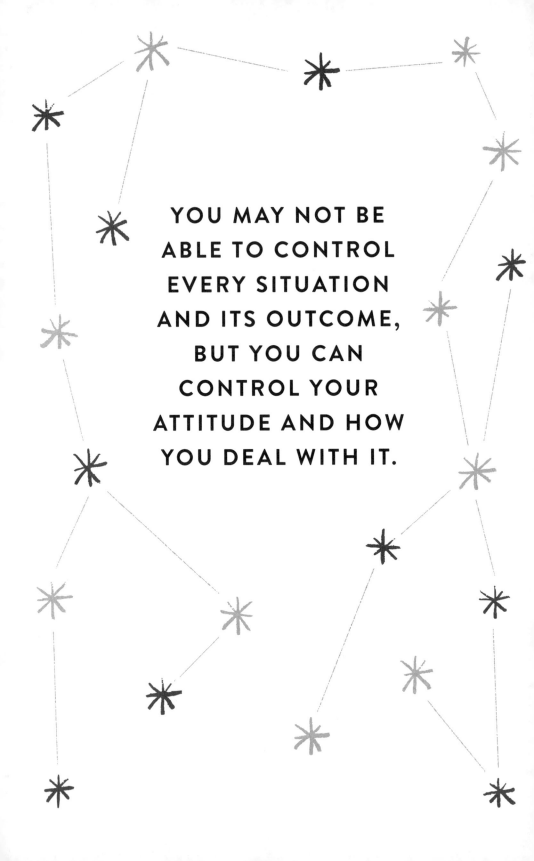

YOU MAY NOT BE
ABLE TO CONTROL
EVERY SITUATION
AND ITS OUTCOME,
BUT YOU CAN
CONTROL YOUR
ATTITUDE AND HOW
YOU DEAL WITH IT.

APRIL

APRIL 1

Do you think telling the truth is always right,
even if it hurts someone's feelings? Explain.

APRIL 2

What are two positive lessons that your
parents taught you as a child?

APRIL 3

Are vacations an important part of your yearly
planning? Why or why not?

APRIL 4

Do you feel comfortable agreeing to
disagree with your friends and family?
Why or why not?

APRIL 5

Are you proud of your job and what you
do for work? Why or why not?

APRIL 6

Do you think you are more of a thinker
or a feeler or a little of both? Do you wish
you were different?

APRIL 7

What does self-care look like to you?
How well do you incorporate self-care
into your life?

APRIL 8

What do you do really, really well?
Does it come naturally or have you
had to work hard at it?

APRIL 9

In your opinion, what is something
that never ends well?

APRIL 10

Why do you think it is important for children
and adults to have role models in their lives?

APRIL 11

If you had to choose to live without
one of your five senses, which one would
you give up and why?

APRIL 12

In regards to past romantic relationships,
what would you do differently if you could do
things all over again?

APRIL 13

Do you have a difficult time setting
limits and boundaries with your family?
Why or why not?

APRIL 14

When you go somewhere new, do you
have an organized plan already mapped out
before you go or do you like to be spontaneous?
Do you like this about yourself? Explain.

APRIL 15

How important is it for you to live
debt-free and why?

APRIL 16

If you got something tattooed on your body,
what would you choose and why?

APRIL 17

Which of your friends do you like spending
time with the most and why?

APRIL 18

What is something you totally geek out
about and are proud to say that you do?

APRIL 19

Are you afraid of death? Why or why not?

APRIL 20

Has anyone ever made you feel uncomfortable sexually? If so, what happened and how did you feel?

APRIL 21

Are you someone who gets easily offended by others? Why or why not?

APRIL 22

What is your favorite way to relax
when things are chaotic?

APRIL 23

What goal have you been putting off
lately and why?

APRIL 24

Would you ever walk up to a stranger and start
a conversation? Why or why not?

APRIL 25

What book has had the greatest impact
on your life and why?

APRIL 26

Growing up, did your parents listen to your
ideas, fears, stories, and feelings? Either way,
how did that make you feel?

APRIL 27

What is the best part and the worst part about
getting older?

APRIL 28

If you stayed at the same job for the next
10 years, would you be okay with that?
Why or why not?

APRIL 29

Why do you think so many couples experience
infidelity and why do you think people cheat?

APRIL 30

What is one personality type that you
typically don't get along with and why?

NEVER BE AFRAID
OF CHANGE.
YOU MAY LOSE
SOMETHING GOOD,
BUT YOU MAY GAIN
SOMETHING EVEN
BETTER.

MAY 1

What do you enjoy about being out
in nature and why?

MAY 2

When someone you care about is upset, what
is the first thing you do? Examples: give them
a hug, listen, help fix the problem, give them
time alone, etc.

MAY 3

Is there anyone you work with that makes you
feel jealous? Why or why not?

MAY 4

What are the qualities of a good listener?

MAY 5

Is there something you need to give up or cut down on and why? Examples: smoking, drinking, TV, phone usage, junk food, etc.

MAY 6

What is something you want to do in the next few months to improve your emotional and/or mental health?

MAY 7

What do you need to do to feel a sense of
accomplishment in life?

MAY 8

What is one failure that has turned
into a great lesson?

MAY 9

Growing up, when you got into trouble, how
did your parents discipline you?

MAY 10

Were any of your past romantic relationships
unhealthy or toxic? Explain.

MAY 11

What do you believe is the purpose of sex
in a romantic relationship?

MAY 12

Are you someone who can stay relatively calm
under pressure? Explain.

MAY 13

If you could be a photographer for a day, what
would you take pictures of and why?

MAY 14

How important is it to you to share the same
religious beliefs with your friends, family, and
romantic relationships? Explain.

MAY 15

When and how did you begin your financial
life independent from your parents?

MAY 16

When you don't forgive someone who has hurt you, how does it affect you? How does it affect the other person?

MAY 17

Have you ever felt judged, ignored, or mistreated because of your gender? Explain.

MAY 18

How did you find out there was no Santa Claus, Easter Bunny, or Tooth Fairy?

MAY 19

What do you think is the first
impression people have meeting you?
Do you think it's accurate?

MAY 20

When you were a teenager, did you
have a solid group of friends or were you
more of a loner?

MAY 21

In your opinion, what is the best way a person
can spend their free time?

MAY 22

Have you ever made a decision that you regret?
What happened?

MAY 23

Have you ever set an unrealistic goal?
What happened?

MAY 24

What do you wish you could tell
yourself five years ago?

MAY 25

Do you think you are reliable in relationships
with others? Why or why not?

MAY 26

Are you someone who is usually early, on
time, or late? Do you like this about yourself?

MAY 27

Do you ever struggle with understanding why
certain people feel the way they feel? Explain.

MAY 28

Have you ever shown a stranger generosity? If so, what did you do and how did it make you feel?

MAY 29

What activity in your life brings you joy?

MAY 30

Why do you think that some people struggle with their sexual identity?

MAY 31

Growing up, when you got hurt or felt scared,
how did your parents comfort you?

TRUE SELF-
DISCOVERY
BEGINS WHERE
YOUR COMFORT
ZONE ENDS.

JUNE

JUNE 1

Growing up, were you someone who enjoyed attending school or did you dread it? Explain.

JUNE 2

Does thinking about the future scare or excite you? Explain.

JUNE 3

If your past boyfriends/girlfriends listed your most negative characteristics, what would they say?

JUNE 4

What is one financial decision you made in the
past that you regret?

JUNE 5

How important is it for you to be involved in
your local community and why?

JUNE 6

When it comes to your physical health,
what is one thing you can work on this year?
What can you do to make it happen?

JUNE 7

Do you make decisions based on how you feel? Why or why not?

JUNE 8

Have you ever witnessed anything in the past that you wish you hadn't? What happened?

JUNE 9

Would you rather have a housekeeper or a chef and why?

JUNE 10

If you could talk to your teenage self,
what would you say?

JUNE 11

Do respect and trust have to be earned in
relationships? Why or why not?

JUNE 12

Think about your first sexual experience.
What sort of feelings did you have? Examples:
safe, loved, abused, awkward, painful,
respected, confusing, etc.

JUNE 13

Do you believe that your parents did the best they could raising you? Why or why not?

JUNE 14

Do you ever struggle with oversharing on social media? Why or why not?

JUNE 15

Are you more of a details person or a big picture person? Explain.

JUNE 16

What would you do with ten million dollars to impact the most amount of people?

JUNE 17

If you could change anything about politics, what would it be and why?

JUNE 18

Do you think of yourself as someone who is emotionally competent? Why or why not?

JUNE 19

Do you ever feel taken advantage of by the people in your life? Explain.

JUNE 20

Do you remember a time when you laughed harder than you've ever laughed? What happened?

JUNE 21

Are you a rule breaker or a rule follower? Have you always been this way? Explain.

JUNE 22

Do you feel comfortable asking family or friends for money? Why or why not?

JUNE 23

When conflict arises in relationships, do you tend to want to face it head-on or avoid it? Explain.

JUNE 24

What kind of legacy do you want to leave behind?

JUNE 25

What is one specific goal you can work towards this week and what is the first step you will take to make it happen?

JUNE 26

When you feel hurt by someone you love, how do you handle that feeling of pain?

JUNE 27

On a scale of 1-10, how much stuff do you tend to keep around (1= a minimalist and 10= a hoarder)? Explain.

JUNE 28

Think about your first crush. Were your feelings towards him/her intense or more mild? Explain.

JUNE 29

In your opinion, what qualities does a healthy, romantic relationship practice?

JUNE 30

Who is your favorite musician, singer, or band? What do you love about their music?

YOU CAN HONOR
YOUR PAST AND
HONOR WHO YOU
ARE BECOMING
FROM IT.

JULY

7

JULY 1

What are some negative thoughts you have
about yourself? When did they start?

JULY 2

What is one goal you have for this year that
you want to accomplish?

JULY 3

In your opinion, which characteristics make
someone reliable?

JULY 4

Who are your core friends and how much time do you think is important to spend with them?

JULY 5

What are some highlights of your adolescent years?

JULY 6

If you see a homeless person on the side of the street, do you think you should give him/her money? Why or why not?

JULY 7

What are some of your talents? Are you utilizing them? How can you use them more?

JULY 8

If you became a teacher for a day, what subject would you feel most confident teaching about and why?

JULY 9

Do you consider yourself a patient person often, sometimes, or rarely? When do you feel the most impatient?

JULY 10

What are some technology boundaries you
want to have in your life and why?

JULY 11

Who is someone you look up to as a mentor
or role model and why?

JULY 12

When was the first time you felt like you were
in love with another person? What happened
in that relationship?

JULY 13

If you could meet anyone, dead or alive, who would it be and why?

JULY 14

Do you consider yourself more of a risk-taker or someone who plays it safe? Have you always been that way? Explain.

JULY 15

What is your first childhood memory?

JULY 16

Has anyone every gossiped about
you that you're aware of? If so, how did
it make you feel?

JULY 17

Do you struggle with comparing yourself to
others? Who do you compare yourself to and
how does that impact you?

JULY 18

In your opinion, what does it look like to be
financially prepared for an emergency?

JULY 19

When things change all of the sudden, do you struggle to be flexible? Why or why not?

JULY 20

What is one country you would like to travel to and why?

JULY 21

Do you tend to think back on the choices you made and wonder if you could have done something different? Why or why not?

JULY 22

When you argue with co-workers,
friends, or family members, what do you
do to try and resolve it?

JULY 23

How would you feel if your life looked exactly
the same one year from now?

JULY 24

Do you remember your first time viewing pornography?
What did you feel physically or emotionally?

JULY 25

What is one personality type that you're
typically drawn to? Explain.

JULY 26

When was a time that you felt creative? What
ended up happening?

JULY 27

When was the most difficult time of your life
and how has that affected you?

JULY 28

What are your family's views on
race and ethnicity? Do you agree with
their views? Why or why not?

JULY 29

Do you feel like you can be assertive with
others? Why or why not?

JULY 30

What are two tangible career goals that you
can set for yourself this coming month?

JULY 31

In this last month, what is one thing you
wished you hadn't committed to and why?

TREAT YOURSELF
WITH LOVE AND
RESPECT AND YOU
WILL ATTRACT
PEOPLE WHO SHOW
YOU LOVE AND
RESPECT.

AUGUST

AUGUST 1

What is something about yourself or your life
that might surprise others to learn?

AUGUST 2

What were some of the challenges you faced
during your adolescent years?

AUGUST 3

Do you believe in life after death? If so,
what do you think it's like?

AUGUST 4

If you could choose any career other than what you do now, what would it be and why?

AUGUST 5

Do you consider yourself a physically affectionate person? Why or why not?

AUGUST 6

Do you ever struggle with blaming others for your mistakes? Why or why not?

AUGUST 7

What causes or movements are you passionate
about and why?

AUGUST 8

How would you rank all the priorities in your life:
work, family, significant other, friends, hobbies,
church, self, school, etc.? Does your ranking reflect
the amount of time you spend on each?

AUGUST 9

What is the difference between failing
and being a failure?

AUGUST 10

When you think about your future, what is
one thing that worries or concerns you?

AUGUST 11

What memories do you have of your
family having fun together?

AUGUST 12

Do you have any fears of abandonment?
Why or why not?

AUGUST 13

What is your most selfish character
trait or habit? What could you do to
change this behavior?

AUGUST 14

What is something you did or didn't do today
that you would love to do every day?

AUGUST 15

Do you tend to be more of an internal
or verbal processor? Have you always
been this way? Explain.

AUGUST 16

Overall, do you believe people tend to be more generous or more stingy with their money? Explain.

AUGUST 17

Have you ever been jealous of someone or something in your life? Explain.

AUGUST 18

What are ways you prefer to spend quality time with the people in your life? Examples: parties, one-on-one, exercising, having dinner together, etc.

AUGUST 19

Have you been minimizing or
stuffing away any memories from your past?
If so, what are you afraid of feeling if you face
those memories?

AUGUST 20

What are your thoughts about mental illness?
Do you think they are treatable?

AUGUST 21

Are you someone who is self-motivated
or do you need accountability? What makes
you this way?

AUGUST 22

When you make mistakes, are you hard
on yourself or do you give yourself grace?
Explain.

AUGUST 23

In your opinion, what makes someone
a good sexual partner?

AUGUST 24

In your opinion, what does the world need
more of and why?

AUGUST 25

If you had an opportunity to go back to school, what subjects would you want to learn about and why?

AUGUST 26

Do you ever feel down and sad for long periods of time? Explain.

AUGUST 27

Were you aware of any feuds or family grudges growing up? Explain.

AUGUST 28

What is one small change you can
make this week that will help you feel in
control of your life?

AUGUST 29

What does being financially comfortable
look like to you?

AUGUST 30

In your opinion, what's the difference between
an insincere and a sincere apology?

AUGUST 31

When it comes to making
life-changing choices, do you use your
head or your heart and why?

LET GO OF WHAT
YOU CANNOT
CHANGE AND
FOCUS ON WHAT
YOU CAN.

SEPTEMBER

SEPTEMBER 1

Do you consider yourself an animal lover?
What is your favorite kind of animal?

SEPTEMBER 2

What excites you about your job and why?

SEPTEMBER 3

What is one bad habit you need to break, but
can't seem to change the behavior? How long
has this been a habit?

SEPTEMBER 4

What is the biggest challenge you face when
you try to set personal goals?

SEPTEMBER 5

Do you get embarrassed easily?
Why do you think that is?

SEPTEMBER 6

Who is someone from your childhood that
showed you a lot of love? What is an example
of what he/she did that made you feel loved?

SEPTEMBER 7

In the last few weeks, did you take
time to practice self-care, rest, and fun?
Why or why not?

SEPTEMBER 8

How does it feel when someone you care
about lies to you?

SEPTEMBER 9

On a scale from 1-10, what is the
highest level of pain you have ever been in?
What happened?

SEPTEMBER 10

What do you miss about being a kid and why?

SEPTEMBER 11

Do you ever pray? If so, how often?

SEPTEMBER 12

Do you consider yourself a generous person most of the time, some of the time, or rarely? Explain.

SEPTEMBER 13

Do you believe crying is a healthy
outlet for negative and positive emotions?
What makes you cry?

SEPTEMBER 14

Do you feel like you have realistic
expectations of others? Why or why not?

SEPTEMBER 15

Why do you think human sex trafficking has
become a worldwide issue?

SEPTEMBER 16

What is your favorite way to learn? Examples:
listen to podcasts, read, watch documentaries,
go to seminars, take classes, etc.

SEPTEMBER 17

Do you feel like you can confide
in your friends about important issues?
Why or why not?

SEPTEMBER 18

When you were a teenager, did you feel more
insecure or more confident? Explain.

SEPTEMBER 19

Why do you believe some people get stuck in their ways, never changing their behaviors?

SEPTEMBER 20

If you could invent an app, what would it do? What would you call it?

SEPTEMBER 21

When you face challenges, do you feel overwhelmed and hopeless or empowered and excited? Explain.

SEPTEMBER 22

When it comes to your emotional
health, what is one thing you want to focus
on this month and why?

SEPTEMBER 23

If you could change anything about religion,
what would it be and why?

SEPTEMBER 24

Do you ever have mood swings or moments
when you tend to be more emotional? Is it
triggered by anything specific?

SEPTEMBER 25

Is social media bringing you closer to your friends and family or making you more isolated and alone? Explain.

SEPTEMBER 26

When you are going through a difficult time, who can you go to that will give you objective feedback to help you process what you are going through? Is there something you need to discuss with that person now?

SEPTEMBER 27

At what age do you want to retire and what type of lifestyle do you want to lead in retirement?

SEPTEMBER 28

What is the difference between
someone who complains and someone
who wants to see change?

SEPTEMBER 29

What do you love about your
personality and why?

SEPTEMBER 30

What are your family's views on politics?
Do you agree with their views? Explain.

HAPPINESS IS
JUST A WORD -
YOU CREATE THE
DEFINITION.

10

OCTOBER

OCTOBER 1

When do you feel the most stubborn and why?

OCTOBER 2

How do you feel about your work schedule last month? Was it too busy, not busy enough, or just right? Explain.

OCTOBER 3

Have you ever taken the time to stand in front of a mirror and explore your body? What are your thoughts and feelings about doing this?

OCTOBER 4

What is something you always love doing, even
when you are tired or overwhelmed?

OCTOBER 5

When you go to your family's house, is there
something they do that makes you feel safe
and loved? Explain.

OCTOBER 6

When you think about the future, what is one
thing that excites you and why?

OCTOBER 7

Are you typically someone who is quick
to accept apologies or do you hold grudges?
Why do you think that is?

OCTOBER 8

Do you tend to meet others' needs
before your own? Explain.

OCTOBER 9

When is a time in your life when you felt
misunderstood by someone? What happened?

OCTOBER 10

If you were the richest person in the world,
what would you do with your time and money?

OCTOBER 11

When do you feel the most insecure? Who are
you with and what is going on?

OCTOBER 12

Growing up, were you ever left out, bullied,
or teased by your peers or family members?
How did that make you feel?

OCTOBER 13

If you had to be on a reality TV show, which
one would you chose and why?

OCTOBER 14

When have you given up on something or
someone? Why did you give up?

OCTOBER 15

What is the most amazing true story
you have ever heard?

OCTOBER 16

How would your best friend describe you?
Do you think you'd agree with his/her
perspective?

OCTOBER 17

What are some things that stress you out
during the holiday season and why? Is there
a way you can better manage or prevent this
stress from happening?

OCTOBER 18

What is your favorite season and why?

OCTOBER 19

How often do you consider how your actions might affect other people before doing something? All of the time, sometimes, or rarely?

OCTOBER 20

What are your thoughts about one-night stands?

OCTOBER 21

How often do you need alone time? How much alone time is too much alone time for you and why?

OCTOBER 22

What is the biggest challenge you face when you try to set career goals?

OCTOBER 23

Is there anything you need to change or give up that would help your relationships thrive?

OCTOBER 24

If you knew you couldn't fail, what would you do?

OCTOBER 25

Do you believe that implementing boundaries
into your life is a form of self-care?
Why or why not?

OCTOBER 26

Are you currently taking anything, or anyone,
for granted? Explain.

OCTOBER 27

When you were a child, were you
complimented or shamed about your looks?
Explain.

OCTOBER 28

What are some behaviors that are
unacceptable during an argument?

OCTOBER 29

Do you think that the more money someone
has, the happier they are? Why or why not?

OCTOBER 30

Do you find yourself distracted easily? Why?

OCTOBER 31

What is a new holiday tradition you would
like to start this year?

PAY MORE
ATTENTION
TO YOUR
INTENTIONS.

NOVEMBER 1

What is your number one financial priority
this month and why?

NOVEMBER 2

When it comes to your family, have you ever
made excuses for their unhealthy behavior(s)?
Why or why not?

NOVEMBER 3

What measures do you think our government
and society could do to help end racism?

NOVEMBER 4

Have you ever made a bucket list of all the things you want to do before you die? Either way, what are some things on your bucket list?

NOVEMBER 5

If you were president for the week, what is one thing you would do differently?

NOVEMBER 6

Would you rather have nosy neighbors or noisy neighbors and why?

NOVEMBER 7

When have you dealt with a conflict
with someone else successfully? What
made it successful?

NOVEMBER 8

Have you ever felt scared or embarrassed to
bring up any questions you had regarding sex and
intimacy to your friends? Why or why not?

NOVEMBER 9

How can you tell if someone is really listening
to what you're saying?

NOVEMBER 10

Would you rather win $50,000 or let your
best friend win $500,000 and why?

NOVEMBER 11

What is the most challenging thing
about your job and why?

NOVEMBER 12

What habits and behaviors do you
do when you feel sad?

NOVEMBER 13

Which of your family members are you closest
to and why? Explain whether you think it's a
healthy relationship or not.

NOVEMBER 14

What are your views on and experiences
with meditation?

NOVEMBER 15

Have your goals in life changed recently?
Why or why not?

NOVEMBER 16

How do your differences help balance out your relationships with others in your life?

NOVEMBER 17

What are two areas of your life that you are insecure about? What is something that you can do to build more confidence in those areas?

NOVEMBER 18

How do your parents handle their money? Do you think they set a good example for you growing up?

NOVEMBER 19

What is one characteristic you received from your parents that you want to keep and one you wish you could change?

NOVEMBER 20

When it comes to alcohol, what do you think is a healthy amount to drink and why?

NOVEMBER 21

Do you feel comfortable asking for help from your friends and family when you feel unsure of something? Why or why not?

NOVEMBER 22

Are you someone who believes that miracles happen? Have you ever experienced or heard of a miraculous story?

NOVEMBER 23

Have you spent time reflecting on your past to help you understand who you are today? Explain.

NOVEMBER 24

Which do you think should have the final say in decision making: logic or emotions? Explain.

NOVEMBER 25

What is your favorite way to celebrate the
holiday season?

NOVEMBER 26

When someone disrespects you, how do you
typically respond? Is your response healthy?

NOVEMBER 27

Do you ever find yourself minimizing your
feelings or the feelings of others? If so, why?

NOVEMBER 28

Do you view boundaries as more restrictive or more protective? Explain.

NOVEMBER 29

Which one of your friends is the most opinionated? Do you butt heads or do you enjoy hearing their opinions?

NOVEMBER 30

In this last month, do you think you spent your free time wisely? Why or why not?

WHEN THINGS
CHANGE INSIDE
OF YOU, THINGS
CHANGE AROUND
YOU.

12

DECEMBER

DECEMBER 1

Do you ever struggle with communicating your needs in relationships? Why or why not?

DECEMBER 2

What habits or addictions have been passed down in your family from previous generations? How has that impacted your life? Examples: alcoholism, mental illness, drug abuse, etc.

DECEMBER 3

In what specific instances have you acted stubbornly? Do you think your stubbornness helped or harmed the situation and why?

DECEMBER 4

What is a charity or non-profit that you would like to give financially to at some point in your life and why?

DECEMBER 5

In your personal life, are you more of a realist or dreamer and why? Does it differ in your work life?

DECEMBER 6

When you create boundaries in relationships, do you have a hard time following through? Why or why not?

DECEMBER 7

Do you believe in God? What does your relationship with God look like?

DECEMBER 8

Would you rather be poor and work at a job you are passionate about or rich and work at a job you absolutely cannot stand? Explain.

DECEMBER 9

Is there an argument that you've had with someone that was never resolved? What can you do to make it better?

DECEMBER 10

Empathy is feeling with someone else. Overall, do you consider yourself an empathetic person? Why or why not?

DECEMBER 11

Do your friends and family members support your goals? Why or why not?

DECEMBER 12

In your opinion, is there anything that should be sexually off-limits?

DECEMBER 13

What is a good thing happening in your life
right now? What makes it good?

DECEMBER 14

Who is the most generous person you've ever
met? Why do you think he/she is so generous?

DECEMBER 15

What makes you angry and what do you do
when you feel angry?

DECEMBER 16

To your best knowledge, how do other
people perceive you?

DECEMBER 17

In your opinion, what makes someone a loyal
friend? Would you consider yourself a loyal
friend? Why or why not?

DECEMBER 18

What would you like said at your funeral?
How do you want to be remembered?

DECEMBER 19

When you were a child and your parents got angry, either with each other or with you, how did it make you feel?

DECEMBER 20

What are some activities or people that make you feel young again?

DECEMBER 21

When making decisions, do you find yourself being more impulsive or cautious and why?

DECEMBER 22

If you were given ten thousand dollars to spend in the next 30 days, how would you spend the money?

DECEMBER 23

What three things can you do regularly to reduce stress in your life?

DECEMBER 24

What is the biggest way you've changed since you were a child? In what way(s) are you still the same?

DECEMBER 25

What is the best gift you have ever received?
What made it so special?

DECEMBER 26

What is something you want to do to improve
your physical health and why?

DECEMBER 27

What one thing do you really want to
purchase but can't afford?

DECEMBER 28

Are you aware of any unhealthy or toxic behaviors that you practiced in your family? Have you implemented boundaries to protect yourself from getting hurt? Why or why not?

DECEMBER 29

Do you always need to be in control? How do you feel when you have no control over a situation?

DECEMBER 30

Do you consider yourself more of a leader or more of a follower and why?

DECEMBER 31

Have you ever made a New Year's resolution?
Why or why not? What was your experience?

NOTES

FEELINGS
WORDS LIST

USE THIS LIST TO HELP YOU EXPLORE YOUR FEELINGS

loved - romantic - appreciative - refreshed - comforted

peaceful - relieved - confident - relaxed - protected

secure - positive - assertive - self-assured - happy

elated - joyful - satisfied - optimistic - delighted

excited - playful - determined - talkative - rejuvenated

ashamed - guilty - embarrassed - stupid - exposed

sad - hopeless - unhappy - crushed - desperate

anxious - uneasy - worried - fearful - indecisive

alone - abandoned - isolated - disconnected

angry - controlled - grumpy - irritated - bitter

confused - misunderstood - deceived - skeptical

exhausted - depressed - withdrawn - lazy - beaten down

overwhelmed - burdened - guarded - tense - confused

INDEX

BOUNDARIES

Jan 5, 24 // **Feb** 10 // **Mar** 4 // **Apr** 7 // **May** 5 // **Jun** 19 // **Jul** 10, 31 // **Aug** 8 // **Sep** 7, 25 // **Oct** 8, 25 // **Nov** 20, 28 // **Dec** 6

CHARACTER & VALUES

Jan 8, 11, 14, 17, 19, 22, 29 // **Feb** 4, 6, 11, 14, 18, 22, 24 // **Mar** 2, 8, 13, 16, 21, 23, 26 // **Apr** 1, 8, 10, 22, 27 // **May** 6, 8, 14, 17, 21, 24, 29 // **Jun** 5, 10, 14, 17, 24 // **Jul** 3, 7, 11, 14, 17, 23, 27 // **Aug** 9, 15, 17, 20, 24, 27, 28 // **Sep** 3, 9, 11, 16, 19, 23, 26 // **Oct** 4, 9, 14, 16, 19, 23, 26 // **Nov** 3, 9, 14, 19, 22, 26, 30 // **Dec** 7, 16, 18, 26, 30

CHILDHOOD & FAMILY

Jan 7, 13, 25 // **Feb** 3, 17, 23 // **Mar** 1, 17, 20, 27 // **Apr** 2, 13, 26 // **May** 9, 20, 31 // **Jun** 1, 13, 28 // **Jul** 5, 15, 28 // **Aug** 2, 11, 19, 27 // **Sep** 6, 18, 30 // **Oct** 5, 12, 27 // **Nov** 2, 13, 23 // **Dec** 2, 19, 24, 28

FEELINGS & PERSONALITY

Jan 6, 12, 20, 23, 26, 31 // **Feb** 1, 8, 16, 20 // **Mar** 5, 11, 19, 28, 31 // **Apr** 6, 14, 19, 21, 24, 30 // **May** 2, 12, 19, 22, 26, 27 // **Jun** 2, 7, 8, 15, 18, 21, 26, 27 // **Jul** 1, 9, 16, 19, 21, 25 // **Aug** 1,

12, 15, 22, 26, 31 // **Sep** 5, 13, 21, 24, 29 // **Oct** 1, 11, 17, 19, 30 // **Nov** 12, 17, 24, 27 // **Dec** 3, 5, 10, 13, 15, 21, 23, 29

GOALS & DREAMS

Jan 4, 27 // **Feb** 26 // **Apr** 3, 23 // **May** 7, 23 // **Jun** 6, 25 // **Jul** 2, 20 // **Aug** 10, 21 // **Sep** 4, 22 // **Oct** 6, 22 // **Nov** 4, 15 // **Dec** 11, 31

JUST FOR FUN

Jan 3, 9, 18, 30 // **Feb** 7, 12, 15, 28 // **Mar** 7, 14, 24 // **Apr** 9, 11, 16, 18, 25 // **May** 1, 13, 18 // **Jun** 9, 20, 30 // **Jul** 8, 13, 26 // **Aug** 3, 14, 25 // **Sep** 1, 10, 20 // **Oct** 13, 15, 18, 31 // **Nov** 5, 6, 10, 25 // **Dec** 8, 20, 25

MONEY & CAREER

Jan 2, 10, 21 // **Feb** 5, 19, 27 // **Mar** 6, 15, 22 // **Apr** 5, 15, 28 // **May** 3, 15, 28 // **Jun** 4, 16, 22 // **Jul** 6, 18, 30 // **Aug** 4, 16, 29 // **Sep** 2, 12, 27 // **Oct** 1, 10, 29 // **Nov** 1, 11, 18 // **Dec** 4, 14, 22, 27

RELATIONSHIPS

Jan 1, 15, 28 // **Feb** 2, 13, 21, 25 // **Mar** 3, 10, 18, 30 // **Apr** 4, 12, 17, 29 // **May** 4, 10, 16, 25 // **Jun** 3, 11, 23, 29 // **Jul** 4, 12, 22, 29 // **Aug** 6, 18, 30 // **Sep** 8, 14, 17, 28 // **Oct** 7, 23, 28 // **Nov** 7, 13, 23, 28 // **Dec** 1, 9, 17

SEXUALITY

Jan 16 // **Feb** 9 // **Mar** 12, 25 // **Apr** 20 // **May** 11, 30 // **Jun** 12 // **Jul** 24 // **Aug** 5, 23 // **Sep** 15 // **Oct** 3, 20 // **Nov** 8 // **Dec** 12

ABOUT
MARRIAGE365

We have a dream that one day happy connected couples will be the norm. Until that day comes, we will continue to work hard to build healthy relationships and bring hope to those who desire to live life to the fullest. That is what gets us up every morning!

That's a lot coming from us, named the couple least likely to succeed in marriage, with a 1.3% chance of making it. By year three of our marriage, we hated each other. Walking our marriage back from the brink of divorce was the most courageous act we have taken. It all started when we stopped waiting for each other to change and instead began the process of self-discovery. We tell every couple that if you want a better relationship, it starts by making a better *you*.

Our restored marriage was the inspiration to help other couples that were feeling stuck, lost, and confused about what to do next. Today, Marriage365 reaches millions of couples around the world, providing practical advice, resources, and inspiration. You can find all of our resources by visiting www.marriage365.com.

Casey and Meygan

Last question for you...

NOW WHAT?

If you found this book helpful, you may be looking for other ways to strengthen your relationship.

Our online **MARRIAGE365 MEMBERSHIP** was created with you in mind. We offer:

- 1000+ Connecting Questions

- Hours of educational webcasts

- Helpful worksheets to build a stronger marriage

- Relationship Checkup

and more...

START YOUR 7-DAY FREE TRIAL AT
marriage365.org/booktrial